GROWING, GOING, GONE

by Vaishali Batra
Illustrated by Kaja Kajfez

Contents

Helpful Plants 2
Plants in Danger 3
Focus on Endangered Plants 6
Houpo Magnolia 7
Big-leaf Mahogany 12
Limestone Cress 15
Monkey Puzzle 19
You Can Help 22
Glossary and Index 24

OXFORD
UNIVERSITY PRESS

Helpful Plants

Plants help us in many ways. They provide food and shelter for people and animals. However, plants need our help too!

There are thousands of **species** of plants on Earth.

Look at all this food!

Plants in Danger

Many plant species are in danger. If we ignore the problem, some species may disappear forever.

Cutting down forests

Plant species can disappear forever when forests are cut down. People cut down forests to make space for farms and cities.

> If you ignore something, you don't take any notice of it. Can you show how you might act if you were ignoring something or someone?

Changes in the atmosphere

Some plant species suffer when the atmosphere changes. If the air gets warmer or drier than before, they cannot grow.

This plant dies if it gets too warm or dry.

The atmosphere is the air around the Earth. How would you feel if the air around you became much hotter and drier?

Pests

Some plants die out when animals move into their **habitat**. Sometimes, animals eat all the plants very quickly – before any new plants can grow. If that happens, the <u>entire</u> plant species might die out.

Possums are considered to be **pests** in some places.

If an <u>entire</u> plant species dies, does that mean every single plant in the species dies, or just some of them?

Focus on Endangered Plants

An endangered plant is a plant that is at risk of dying out. We are going to look at four different endangered plants.

houpo magnolia

big-leaf mahogany

limestone cress

monkey puzzle

Houpo Magnolia

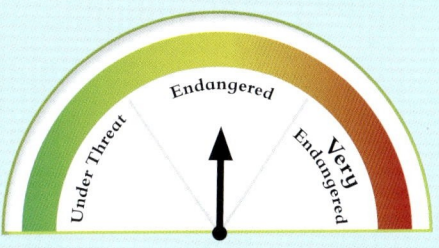

Houpo magnolia trees grow on mountains in China.

How tall do they grow?
20 metres

How long do they live?
100 years

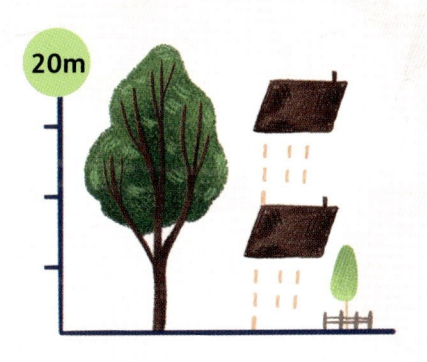

20m

Fascinating fact: They have beautiful flowers that smell nice.

Lots of the forests where houpo magnolias live have been cut down. The land is now used for farming. This means houpo magnolias have lost nearly their entire habitat.

houpo magnolia bark

For thousands of years, people have also peeled off the tree bark to make medicines to treat coughs and colds.

Magnolia bark medicine

Without its bark to protect it, a houpo magnolia tree can easily get a disease and die.

a sick houpo magnolia

What might be a <u>difference</u> between how a sick houpo magnolia tree looks, and how a healthy houpo magnolia tree looks?

10

Conservationists are working to save houpo magnolias. They carefully grow lots of new houpo magnolia trees. Then they plant the young trees in forests.

This is a way to grow new plants from old plants.

Big-leaf Mahogany

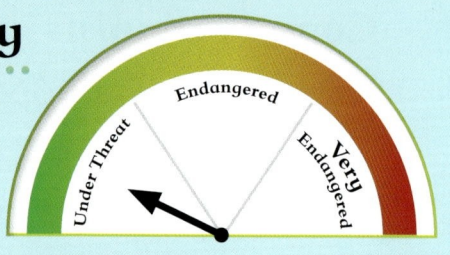

Big-leaf mahogany trees are also endangered. They grow in Central and South America.

How tall do they grow?
60 metres

How long do they live?
350 years

Fascinating fact:
They are called big-leaf mahogany trees because their leaves can grow up to 50 centimetres long!

60m

These trees are cut down for their **timber**. The timber is used to make <u>fine</u> quality furniture and musical instruments.

Mahogany furniture is very <u>fine</u> quality. Does that mean it is very good, or that it is not very good?

13

Some countries in South America are helping the big-leaf mahogany trees. They have set limits on the number of trees that can be cut down.

This big-leaf mahogany tree is safe!

Limestone Cress

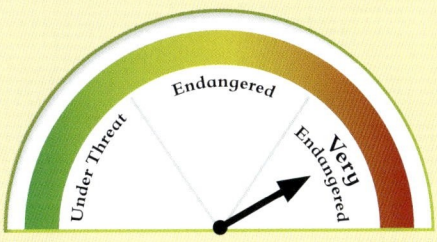

Limestone cress plants are very rare. They only grow in the Waitaki Valley in New Zealand, on a type of rock called limestone.

*Under Threat / Endangered / **Very Endangered***

How tall do they grow?
10 centimetres

Fascinating fact: In 2005, only 21 limestone cress plants survived in the wild.

New Zealand

Waitaki Valley

limestone cress

Limestone cress plants are endangered because of the arrival of pests, like rabbits, in their habitat. Rabbits love eating limestone cress!

The arrival of pests has caused problems for the limestone cress. Does 'arrival' mean that the pests have come to live there, or that they have gone away?

Weeds also make it difficult for the limestone cress to grow because they take up all the space!

They need pulling up!

Conservationists are helping limestone cress plants by removing weeds. They are also building fences around the limestone cress' habitat, to keep pests out.

Keep out, rabbits!

Monkey Puzzle

Monkey puzzle trees grow on mountains in Chile and Argentina.

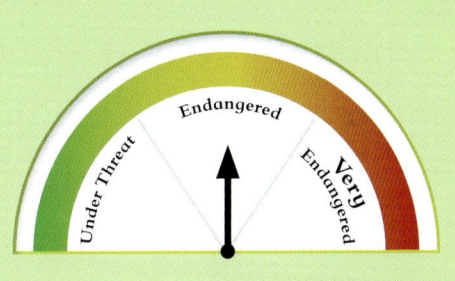

Endangered · Under Threat · Very Endangered

How tall do they grow?
50 metres

50m

How long do they live?
Over 1000 years!

Fascinating fact:
Monkey puzzle trees were around at the same time as the dinosaurs.

19

People cut down a lot of monkey puzzle trees. They use monkey puzzle timber to make things like buildings and bridges.

Forest fires can destroy the trees' entire habitat too.

Monkey puzzle timber is strong.

monkey puzzle bark

Lots of monkey puzzle trees are now grown in nature **reserves**. In reserves, no one can cut them down. This helps to make sure that monkey puzzle trees do not die out.

South America

Chile

These trees are in a nature reserve in Chile.

21

You Can Help

Once a plant is extinct, it is gone forever.
We cannot <u>ignore</u> the need to save endangered plants. We need to care for them now!

Experts are teaching people to care for endangered plants. What do you think will happen if we <u>ignore</u> their advice?

Just like a conservationist, you can make a difference too. You can find out more about endangered plants. Perhaps you could raise money for a **charity** that helps them?

You can start today!

Glossary

charity: an organization that raises money to help people or nature

conservationists: people working to protect nature

habitat: the place where a plant or an animal lives

pest: an insect, animal, or plant that causes damage to things

reserves: places where animals and plants are protected

species: a group of related animals or plants

timber: wood used to make something

weeds: wild plants that grow where you do not want them to

Index

conservationist 11, 18, 23
endangered 6, 12, 15, 16, 19, 22–23
extinct 22
food 2
shelter 2